the flap pamph ⌐ᴜs

The Courtesans Reply

open, read, turn

The Courtesans Reply

the flap pamphlet series (No. 7)
Printed and Bound in the United Kingdom

Published by the flap series, 2012
the pamphlet series of flipped eye publishing
All Rights Reserved

Cover Design by Petraski
Series Design © flipped eye publishing, 2010
Author Photo © Ania Tomaszeska-Nelson

First Edition

Thanks are due to the editors of the following publications in which
some of these poems, or earlier versions of them, have appeared:
Modern Poetry in Translation 3:12 (2009)
Modern Poetry in Translation 3:13 (2010)
Ten: New Poets from Spread the Word (Bloodaxe, 2010)

ISBN-13: 978-1-905233-40-3

LOTTERY FUNDED

The Courtesans Reply

Shazea Quraishi

Contents | *The Courtesans Reply*

"How wonderful is the supreme beauty of Kusumapura!
Here, between the rows of houses the streets are well-watered,
well-cleaned, and are scattered over with flower-offerings great and small...
Daughters of courtezans, the beauty of whose lotus-like faces is being drunk
by the eyes of all people, are gracefully walking up and down,
it seems, to bestow their favour on the thoroughfare."

from *The UBHAYABHISARIKA*
translated by Manomohan Ghosh

The Sixty-Four Arts

Of pleasant disposition,
beautiful and otherwise attractive,
master of sixty-four arts:
music, dancing, acting, singing,
the composition of poetry,
flower-arrangement and garland-making,
the preparation of perfumes,
cosmetics, dress-making, embroidery, conjuring,
sleight of hand,
logic, cooking, sorcery, fencing
with sword and staff,
archery, gymnastics, carpentry,
chemistry, architecture
and mineralogy,
the composition of riddles, tongue-twisters
and other puzzles, gardening, writing in cipher,
languages, making artificial flowers
and clay modelling,
training fighting cocks, partridges
and rams, teaching parrots and mynah-birds to talk...
Such a courtesan will be honoured by the King, praised
by the learned, and all will seek her favours
and treat her with consideration.

Tambulasena

In the beginning
my whole body was covered with skin
hard as rock. Then he came

and his mouth
running over me was a river, cool and quick,
with small silver fish.

Night after night
he shaped me,
smoothed me down

to velvet
bones.

*

Now I bathe while he watches,
eyes fireflies
on my skin.

I bend over,
my hair between us
a curtain of water.

I let him towel me dry,
his strokes soft... then brisk,
a cloth shining a lamp.

Water drips down
my back. He grasps my hair
and climbs.

Vanarajika
speaks of the eight varieties of nail marks

Using the nail on my middle finger
I mark his neck
with a half moon, on the place
I like best
to kiss.
A sign of my devotion.

      On his lower belly, I leave
      a circle.

            Often I trace a short, straight line
            on his chest
            his belly
            his back.
            The dash.

                Lightly, he touches my cheek
                giving me gooseflesh,
                then marks me with his thumb,
                deepening the scratch with the other fingers.
                A knife stroke.

On my buttocks,
a mark resembling a lotus leaf.

The peacock's claw is for me alone.
The hare's jump even more.

The tiger's claw
he traces under my breast
binds me to him.

Ramadasi

Return
to me, beloved
and take me on your lap.

Undo my braid,
stiff
as buffalo horn

and draw your
fingers
through my hair.

Untie my belt, open
the silk cloth
covering my waist,

let my oiled limbs, my
perfumed skin
envelop you

as the rose
swallows
the bee.

The Days of Chandragupta Maurya

were split into sixteen hours
of ninety minutes each.

In the first, he arose
and prepared himself by meditation;
in the second, he studied
the reports of his agents
and issued secret instructions;
he met with his councillors in the third hour
and, in the fourth, attended to state
finances and national defence;
in the fifth, he heard the petitions
and suits of his subjects.
In the sixth hour, he bathed
dined and read religious literature.
In the seventh hour, while he made official appointments,
he received taxes and tribute.
In the eighth, he met his council again,
heard the reports of his spies and courtesans.
The ninth hour was devoted to relaxation
and prayer,
the tenth and eleventh given to military matters
and the twelfth to secret reports.
In the thirteenth hour, the king indulged
in an evening bath and a meal,
and for the next three hours he slept...

but never in the same bed twice.

Sukumarika

to Ramasena

My dearest, my life,
moon to my night,
remember our happiness?

Recall, if you can,
the equal kiss, *Sama,*
and the pressed kiss, *Pidita.*
Aschita, the devouring kiss
and *Mridu,* the delicate kiss…
Also, the inflamer,
the kiss of encouragement,
the awakening kiss,
the vagabond, the joyful
kiss, the vibrant one,
the bowed kiss, the twisted kiss and
the satisfied kiss.

Have you forgotten
the taste of my mouth
sweetened with betel?
My garments, outer and inner,
white as milk.
The sound of my bangles
during love, their silence
in sleep.

Remember my lips
nibbling,
pinching,
kissing,
browsing,
sucking the mango,
devouring.

Remember
the way I make you feel — like twenty men —
     and in your hands
     my painted feet.

Priyangusena
speaks of the Keeper of the King's Zoo

He is not like other men.
He prefers me unperfumed,
likes to watch me

remove hair flowers,
undo the *rasana*
around my waist.

In the morning I am porcupine,
at night, Dhole,
four-horned antelope.

He tells me secrets
of the Nilgai, its fondness
for almonds,

how the Chinkara leaps
the palace walls
and back again.

Ratisena

to Chandragupta Maurya

While you sleep, I take
your white shirt
from the unpainted chair,
smoothe it with my hands
the way I smoothe
          the tiredness from your body,
                    pressing my self against you.
                              Sh...

Let me take your worries,
your secrets - those sharp
small stones you carry
with you always.

I know you have women half my age
— I see them in the street, swaying
like long grass, their *saris*
concealing slim legs
that circled your waist.

Are you my King
or the boy I met at the well
so many summers past?

I watch you sleeping.
My small bed cradles you,
my only child,
my only man.

Messenger

Malatika remembers you.
Her passion, hundred-petalled,
grows and grows, eclipsing all flowers
in her mother's garden: lotus, marigold,
raat-ki-rani, rose.

Each day she strokes her skin
with perfumed oil,
each day she adorns her self
with pleasing things.
And as she walks, thinking of you,
her ankle-bracelets sound,
a hundred tiny, silver bells
trembling.

Madhavesana

Once more this
pressing of bodies, his desire
beating against me as the eagle's wings
against the air that lifts him up, up.

My body has learned to soften
and bend, but my heart,
child who will not listen, clings
to a soft, grubby thing.

After I have washed the sweat,
the trails of saliva from my skin,
I stand at the open window,
let the breeze dry my face.

Sondasi

I smile slow as honey,

offer him
my pollen-dusted breasts.
I press my nose to his skin,
smell Varunika on him.

     Wait

the word a caress,
I undress him
— the first time I have done this.

§

The next day
she is not with him.

I seat him on the low, green chair,
move in his lap
put my mouth to his ear:

     Tell me what you do with her

He answers
and I show him
the flame lit inside me.

§

Varunika,
queen of forests.

Her teeth
marks on his lips,
her nail marks on his back,

      her love note to me.

§

A dark pink flower falls
from her hair as she passes
— I hold it carefully in my hand: five petals,
one scattered with small, dark markings.

Opening it, I stroke the velvet
inside, eleven stamens raise
their pollen-tipped nubs
to the tip of my tongue.

Pradymnadasi
on biting

When he gave me the discreet bite on my lower lip,
I sighed with disappointment,
knowing his mark would fade.

The coral jewel bite he bestowed on my left breast,
then the right. Around my neck
he placed a necklace of gems.

I will wear no ornaments today other than kiss
marks on my ears, filigree
bites on my hot, hot cheeks.

Before he left, he gave me the bite I like best:
the nibbling of the wild boar.
　　　　　And so, he knew I would wait.

Devadatta

I'm summoned to the jasmine terrace
where he waits
reclining on the large, low bed
draped in blues and reds and oranges.

He's with Sondasi's servant girl
— her gaze is lowered, his
rests on her breasts, where a blush blooms
above her open blouse.

Her waist is a handspan, her hips
high and wide.
During the love act, he moves my legs
to one side

so she will see as he enters me.
He doesn't look at me,
but, over my shoulder, watches her
small, heart-shaped face.

ndasi

Tell me I am necessary for you like sleep,
not like opium which carries forgetting,
or pleasant as a breeze
scented with jasmine.

Tell me what you see
behind my art, my bright cloth.
Look into my face and show it to me.

Tell me what you read in books
and hear in coffee houses,
at wedding parties. Teach me.

When our tired, gladdened bodies
drift onto the bed,
kiss me like a husband
and spread over me an endless blue wing…

Anangadatta

Dreams I have —

The peaceful routine of household chores:
       sweeping the floors of the house,
              sprinkling water on the yellow earth outside the door.

Cooking my husband's food,
       anticipating his pleasure.

Feeding sweet, milky pudding to my child.
       Sewing a button on my husband's shirt.

To spend the whole night dreaming,
       my child pressed against my back,
              my husband's breath in my hair.

Epilogue

How is a man to know whether
a courtesan has a passion for him?

Side-long glances,
smiling,
a frown brightening her face,
adding gestures to complete the sense of words,
sudden and short laughter with the clapping of hands,
exposing the navel, arm-pits and breasts,
and touching the *mekhala*...
all these indicate that a woman is struck
by the arrows of the god of love.

How can scratching and biting,
even if they are painful, create pleasure?

Just as a whip
when used by the charioteer,
makes horses mindful of speed,
so the use of nails and teeth
during intercourse
engross the heart in the pleasure of touch.

Tell more of the art of scratching...

When a man sees, even from afar,
nail marks on a girl's breasts,
he feels interest and desire for her
even without knowing her.

And it often happens,
when a woman sees nail marks
on the various parts of a man's body,
her spirit awakens
            and takes her to him.

How is a courtesan to choose?

Here is a list of men to be avoided:

Those with tuberculosis,
with worms in their excrement,
with bad breath,
in love with their wife,
coarse in word,
brutal,
cruel,
abandoned by their parents,
insensitive to praise and insult,
immodest,
frequenting enemies for hope of gain...
Also one who is a thief,
an idiot
or one who practises magic.

How is a man to conciliate
a woman whom he has offended?

After considering all means of pacifying her anger
— grasping her feet,
swearing repeatedly,
making her laugh by any means whatsoever -
we recommend kissing her forcibly
because this yields the proper result at once.

> The great joy which arises
> from kissing forcibly
> the mouth of the dear woman in question
> — after grasping in your left hand
> her hair perfumed with incense,
> and catching her two hands in your right hand -
> will increase passion,
> even in an old man,
> and will stop his ageing.

Notes &
Acknowledgements

The Courtesans Reply is a work of fiction. The first and last lines of **Carandasi** are quotes from the poem 'Two stranger birds in our feathers' by Mahmoud Darwish. The **Epilogue** employs found text from *'Glimpses of Sexual Life in Nanda-Maurya India: a translation of the Caturbhāṇī*, translated by Manomohan Ghosh (Manisha Granthalaya Private Ltd, Calcutta, 1975) and from *'The Complete Kāma Sūtra*, translated by Alain Daniélou (Park Street Press, 1994).

Acknowledgements

I am indebted to Manomohan Ghosh for his book 'Glimpses of Sexual Life in Nanda Maurya India', which inspired this work. I am also grateful to Alain Daniélou's translation of 'The Complete Kāma Sūtra (Park Street Press, 1994), an invaluable source of reference and material. Warmest thanks to Mimi Khalvati and Stephen Knight for their wise and generous guidance, to The Complete Works Programme (Spread the Word 2008-2010), and to Sarojini Arinayagam for a calm, quiet place.

Lightning Source UK Ltd.
Milton Keynes UK
UKOW03f2124110214

226311UK00003B/62/P